Go to http://www.businessconnectionexpert.com
to get your complimentary copy of
*52 Ways to Leverage LinkedIn -
Making Your Connections Count.*

Converting Connections to Ca$h & Relationships to Revenue

Connections That Count

Rhonda Sher

THiNKaha®

An Actionable Business Journal

E-mail: info@thinkaha.com
20660 Stevens Creek Blvd., Suite 210
Cupertino, CA 95014

Published by THiNKaha®
20660 Stevens Creek Blvd., Suite 210, Cupertino, CA 95014
http://thinkaha.com
E-mail: info@thinkaha.com

First Printing: July 2018
Hardcover ISBN: 978-1-61699-272-9 1-61699-272-7
Paperback ISBN: 978-1-61699-271-2 1-61699-271-9
eBook ISBN: 978-1-61699-273-6 1-61699-273-5
Place of Publication: Silicon Valley, California, USA
Paperback Library of Congress Number: 2018947690

Trademarks

Warning and Disclaimer

Acknowledgement

I believe that giving someone an acknowledgment is one of the best ways to connect with them. There are so many people I have connected with in my life who have had a positive impact on me and made my life so much better. If I have not mentioned you by name, please know that I appreciate our connection and my life is so much better because of it.

I want to thank my amazing husband, Bob Sher, who has always believed in me, supported me, loved me, and been there for me, no matter the circumstances. Bob is my husband and "wasband," since we were married for twenty-eight years, divorced for six years, and remarried two-and-a-half years ago. He is, and always has been, there for me, and for that, I will always be grateful. Thank you for supporting my dreams and being my partner in creating our future and the new connections we have yet to make.

I also want to thank my amazing daughters, Stefanie and Vanessa, for being the strong, smart, beautiful young women that they are. They have been my greatest teachers, and I have learned more from them than they will ever know. I acknowledge them for all they have done and continue to do in the world and for allowing me to have the privilege of being their mom. I love you both more than you will ever know.

Thank you to all the friends in my personal development community who have supported and connected with me. From you, I have truly learned what it is to be part of a community and live in a world where anything is possible.

Thank you to all the people who contributed to this book in any way. Thank you for your AHA Thoughts, for your support and generosity of time in making this book a reality.

To all my LinkedIn connections, many of whom I consider to be friends, thank you for being part of my circle and for your contributions. Without your connections, I would not be who I am today.

To all my friends, past and present, and to those future friends and connections I have yet to meet, thank you for showing up in my life and for your presence. I know that without connection, life is very lonely. Connection is truly a way we can touch, move, and inspire others to reach our dreams. For all those people who have touched, moved, and inspired me to create this book, thank you for your connection.

Thank you, Mitchell Levy, and your amazing AHAthat staff for helping me to make this book a reality.

I am truly grateful for the opportunity to be part of the AHAthat platform and to be able to share the importance and power of connection. When we connect with another person, magic happens. I hope that you can find those connections that will bring you light, love, and magic. I am grateful for all of the people in my life.

Dedication

This book is dedicated to all my connections, past, present, and future. I appreciate you. Some connections last a day and some connections last a lifetime. It is not the amount of time that a connection lasts, but the imprint it leaves on your heart. It has been proven by research that connecting with others is good for our moods and even our physical health. Real connections are more than just talking with others or sharing interests. They can happen anywhere, sometimes without anything being said.

A true connection happens when you are in the moment, you are being yourself; there is a sense of trust that exists between you and the other person, and you feel empathy or kindness toward the other person. Connections can also grow from something as simple as a smile, an online invitation, or a phone call. They can happen instantly or grow over time. That is the beautiful thing about connections—they happen in many ways.

If we have not yet connected, feel free to reach out on LinkedIn and connect with me. This book is dedicated to you. https://www.LinkedIn.com/in/RhondaLSher

How to Read a THiNKaha® Book
A Note from the Publisher

The THiNKaha series is the CliffsNotes of the 21st century. The value of these books is that they are contextual in nature. Although the actual words won't change, their meaning will change every time you read one as your context will change. Experience your own "AHA!" moments ("AHAmessages™") with a THiNKaha book; AHAmessages are looked at as "actionable" moments—think of a specific project you're working on, an event, a sales deal, a personal issue, etc. and see how the AHAmessages in this book can inspire your own AHAmessages, something that you can specifically act on. Here's how to read one of these books and have it work for you:

1. Read a THiNKaha book (these slim and handy books should only take about 15–20 minutes of your time!) and write down one to three actionable items you thought of while reading it. Each journal-style THiNKaha book is equipped with space for you to write down your notes and thoughts underneath each AHAmessage.

2. Mark your calendar to re-read this book again in 30 days.

3. Repeat step #1 and write down one to three more AHAmessages that grab you this time. I guarantee that they will be different than the first time. BTW: this is also a great time to reflect on the actions taken from the last set of AHAmessages you wrote down.

After reading a THiNKaha book, writing down your AHAmessages, re-reading it, and writing down more AHAmessages, you'll begin to see how these books contextually apply to you. THiNKaha books advocate for continuous, lifelong learning. They will help you transform your ahas into actionable items with tangible results until you no longer have to say "AHA!" to these moments—they'll become part of your daily practice as you continue to grow and learn.

As The AHA Guy at THiNKaha, I definitely practice what I preach. I read 2-3 AHAbooks a month in addition to those that we publish and take away two to three different action items from each of them every time. Please e-mail me your AHAs today!

Mitchell Levy
publisher@thinkaha.com

THiNKaha®

Contents

Introduction

One of my favorite authors, Sam Horn, had a quote in her book, *Got Your Attention*, from her mom, Ruth Reed, that really says it all about the power of connection: "Connecting is not a spectator sport."

As an author, speaker, entreprencur, LinkedIn expert, connector, wife, and mother, I know that one of the most important skills someone can master is how to connect with others. The best way to do that is by conversing with someone. That is not as easy as it sounds, since most of us were brought up being taught NOT to talk to strangers. At the same time, we were also NOT taught how to be good listeners. If this is the case, then how can we become powerful connectors? After all, in the business world, it is NOT who you know, but who knows you. If you don't talk to strangers and know how to listen in a way that someone feels heard, then how can you connect powerfully with another person? In this book, I have shared some of the most powerful ways to make real connections that can impact your life on a positive note, both personally and professionally.

Did you know that goldfish have a longer attention span than humans do? This surprising fact is from the acclaimed Harvard Business School researcher, Nancy F. Koehn. If that is true, then making a connection can be a daunting task, since you need to get someone's attention to make a connection with them. If you really want to make powerful connections with others, you need to be able to keep that person's favorable attention and gift them with yours. In this book, I have shared some of the best ways I know to make the connection with others. I have also asked some of my connections to share their best thoughts on how to connect.

Today, more than ever, in a world where communication and connection are done on a mobile device or computer, the ability to connect on a deep, powerful level is more challenging than ever.

Author Lou Solomon said it best with the quote, "Human connection is an energy exchange between people who are paying attention to one another. It has the power to deepen the moment, inspire change, and build trust."

I invite you to have at least one deep, powerful conversation a day to make those connections. Let's connect on LinkedIn as well. You can find me at https://LinkedIn.com/in/RhondaLSher.

To create an endless pipeline of connections, do what your mother told you not to do: Talk to strangers and master the "F" word – Follow-up.
http://aha.pub/RhondaSher

Rhonda L. Sher
http://aha.pub/ConvertingConnections

Share the AHA messages from this book socially by going to
http://aha.pub/ConvertingConnections.

Section I

Business Connections Are Invaluable

Everyone has the ability to connect with others to create meaningful business connections, although not everyone has the skills. The good news is that these skills can be learned. The key is a servant leadership mindset. Listen to others, and either solve or recommend a solution they can use to solve their pain point. Spend the time to build relationships that last.

1

Read and share amazing AHAmessages from "Converting Connections to Ca$h & Relationships to Revenue" http://aha.pub/ConvertingConnections. http://aha.pub/RhondaSher

_____

_____

2

Many of us try to silence the pain of disconnection by being over-busy, over-eating, spending too much time on social media, or anything that alters our mood. Making meaningful connections means being intentional and in the moment. http://aha.pub/RhondaSher

_____

_____

3

Be crystal clear about what you do in your business to attract your ideal clients. When asked what you do, say, "My clients hire me to [fill in the blank] because I [state the problem you solve]. What kind of clients do you work with?" http://aha.pub/RhondaSher

_____

_____

4

My goal is to help the speakers we represent to connect with audience members & provide incredible value with cutting-edge information & resources and to be the best version of themselves! -Shelly Harrison, Publicist via http://aha.pub/RhondaSher

_____

_____

5

When you meet somebody for the first time, put the focus on them. Ask questions to learn what's important to them and how you can be a resource. That's how a connection can begin. http://aha.pub/RhondaSher

_____

_____

6

Simply exchanging business cards does not make a connection. Connections are made when there is a conversation and the person you are talking to has your full attention and interest. Ask questions and really listen.
http://aha.pub/RhondaSher

_____

_____

7

You will become like the five people you associate with the most. This can be either a blessing or a curse. -Billy Cox
via http://aha.pub/RhondaSher

_____

_____

8

Business connections are built on relationships based on "know, like, and trust." Remember, people want to work with those they feel a connection to. http://aha.pub/RhondaSher

_____

_____

9

People want to work with others who give positive vibrations. Smile often, and with your body language let others know you are approachable and want to connect.
http://aha.pub/RhondaSher

10

Technology has helped us connect to people in ways that were never possible before. The downside is, we are often disconnected from our souls and passions. Spend 24 hours completely disconnected from technology and watch the connections that happen.
http://aha.pub/RhondaSher

11

A powerful question to ask to find out what people want is, "If I could grant you one wish in business, what would it be?"
http://aha.pub/RhondaSher

_____

_____

12

Business connections that last are built on friendship. Build strong friendships and you will always have great connections.
http://aha.pub/RhondaSher

_____

_____

13

To create an endless pipeline of connections, do what your mother told you not to do: Talk to strangers and master the "F" word -- Follow-up.
http://aha.pub/RhondaSher

_____

_____

14

Treat celebrities like regular people and treat regular people like celebrities. You will be amazed at the reactions that you receive and how easy it will be to make a connection. http://aha.pub/RhondaSher

_____

_____

15

If your business comes from relationships, relationships should be your business. -Doug Ales via http://aha.pub/RhondaSher

_____

_____

16

Make sure you meet at least one new person a week. By doing so, you begin building a larger network of business connections. Being connected to groups of people will increase your visibility and your odds of finding new opportunities. http://aha.pub/RhondaSher

_____

_____

17

Once you make a connection to another person, make sure to keep the connection alive by keeping in touch. -Gladys Edmonds via http://aha.pub/RhondaSher

_____

_____

18

Remember the Boy Scout motto:
BE PREPARED. Always bring business cards.
Connections can be made anywhere:
at a store, waiting for your order at a cafe,
on vacation, etc. You never know where
your next great connection will happen.
http://aha.pub/RhondaSher

_____

_____

People feel at ease, warm up, and connect with you when they realize that you really want to learn more about and help them. http://aha.pub/RhondaSher

Rhonda L. Sher
http://aha.pub/ConvertingConnections

Share the AHA messages from this book socially by going to
http://aha.pub/ConvertingConnections.

Section II

Developing Heart-to-Heart Connections

Making great connections with people isn't about who you know, it's about who knows you. You need to show up as the "real" you, and you need to care about the person you're talking with. You should be talking far less than you're listening. When those you're connecting with see that your passion, energy, and focus are on them, they will open up to you. This section will give you ways to turn simple conversations into real connections.

19

Making great connections with people isn't about who you know, it's about who knows you. Make yourself someone who is interesting to others by being genuinely interested in those you meet. http://aha.pub/RhondaSher

_____

_____

20

Invest more time into fewer relationships. That may sound counterintuitive. Generally, your networking effect is far stronger since people who have deeper relationships with you create more powerful referral relationships on your behalf. http://aha.pub/RhondaSher

---

21

When we know ourselves to be connected to all others, acting compassionately is simply the natural thing to do. -Rachel Naomi Remen via http://aha.pub/RhondaSher

---

22

Connection is about standing out from all the noise and actually doing what you say and saying what you do. When people know that you keep your commitments, they will trust you, and that's when deeper connections form. http://aha.pub/RhondaSher

_____

_____

23

You can make connections by getting people curious. Bring a book with you or wear a name tag, logo, sweater, shirt, or something that catches their attention.
http://aha.pub/RhondaSher

_____

_____

24

If you want deeper connections, care about the people who are in your life. Know intimately what matters to them.
http://aha.pub/RhondaSher

_____

_____

25

If you want people to open up while connecting with them, make it a point to ask open-ended questions that allow them to reveal more about themselves. Then follow up with pertinent questions. http://aha.pub/RhondaSher

---

26

A powerful way to connect with someone is knowing intimately what their "why" is (in other words, what makes them tick). http://aha.pub/RhondaSher

---

27

Real & meaningful connections are always
there: the associate who has or will find an
answer or the friend who offers a safe space,
w/ non-judgmental support, assistance,
creativity & knowledge. -Sue Urda, Cofounder
of Powerful You! Women's Network
via http://aha.pub/RhondaSher

_____

_____

28

Look for areas of commonality in the people you meet. Acknowledge them for something they've done or handled well. A compliment is one of the greatest ways to open a conversation. http://aha.pub/RhondaSher

_____

_____

29

Connecting with someone is not necessarily a bond with a significant other, or even a friend, but can be the indefinable -- perhaps the rarest and most precious thing in life to find at all. -Donna Lynn Hope via http://aha.pub/RhondaSher

_____

_____

30

Make it a habit to like, share, or compliment someone every day.
http://aha.pub/RhondaSher

_____

_____

31

When making a connection with somebody for the first time, be interested, not interesting. Ask, "What do you love about your life or your business?" instead of, "What do you do?" http://aha.pub/RhondaSher

_____

_____

32

The history of your happiness is the history of
your feeling connected. -Vironika Tugaleva
via http://aha.pub/RhondaSher

_____

_____

33

There is no exercise better for the heart than
reaching down and lifting people up.
-John Andres Holmes
via http://aha.pub/RhondaSher

_____

_____

34

Phones and tablets are huge distractions. When you are talking with someone, avoid the temptation to break eye contact, and ignore digital distractions. Your full attention is one of the greatest gifts you can give to someone. http://aha.pub/RhondaSher

_____

_____

35

Real connections are made person to person. If you have the option, always choose face-to-face. You can never replace human interaction. http://aha.pub/RhondaSher

_____

_____

36

Actions speak louder than words. Practice
being kind and caring with others.
When they see you as a person who cares,
they'll want to be associated with you.
http://aha.pub/RhondaSher

_____

_____

37

Connections are never random. They are almost always connected to a greater purpose.
http://aha.pub/RhondaSher

_____

_____

38

Connections are good for us on a spiritual level because we crave community and acceptance. There's something in our soul that feels good when we cultivate healthy relationships.
http://aha.pub/RhondaSher

_____

_____

39

Don't wait for extraordinary opportunities.
Take ordinary things and make them
extraordinary. http://aha.pub/RhondaSher

40

It is not always easy to step out of your comfort zone and connect with someone. However, when you reach out, make a connection, and develop a relationship, you create comfortable connections from that point forward. http://aha.pub/RhondaSher

_____

_____

41

Dale Carnegie once said, "Remember that a person's name is, to that person, the sweetest and most important sound in any language." Remembering someone's name and using it in conversation is just as powerful now. http://aha.pub/RhondaSher

_____

_____

42

If you are stressed when you're going to meet new people, take a moment to breathe and get centered. Being in a positive frame of mind makes it easier to connect.
http://aha.pub/RhondaSher

_____

_____

43

Consider working with a business coach. This can "fast-forward" your ability to create relationships that matter.
http://aha.pub/RhondaSher

_____

_____

44

Focus on building people and you will build your business. http://aha.pub/RhondaSher

_____

_____

When you connect with someone, it is important to keep up with them. Nurturing true connections is important because they're based on relationships. Communicating regularly keeps connections alive.
http://aha.pub/RhondaSher

Rhonda L. Sher
http://aha.pub/ConvertingConnections

Share the AHA messages from this book socially by going to
http://aha.pub/ConvertingConnections.

Section III

It's Better to Give Than to Receive

It's better to give than to receive. There is never a truer statement in regard to making connections. Give first and when appropriate, you will receive. Initiating meaningful relationships requires work: it's about practicing the art of giving before receiving. By following the thoughts in this section, you will start to build deep, lasting connections with others that will pay dividends for years.

45

The more you give to others, the more you receive in return. Make it a practice to do random acts of kindness.
http://aha.pub/RhondaSher

_____

_____

46

Making a connection is not about impressing someone, it is about creating intrigue and interest. Once that is established, the connection will follow. http://aha.pub/RhondaSher

_____

_____

47

Everything is connected. The connections that truly matter involve being present, listening actively, and demonstrating to the person you're with that they matter to you.
http://aha.pub/RhondaSher

_____

_____

48

People feel at ease, warm up, and connect with you when they realize that you really want to learn more about and help them.
http://aha.pub/RhondaSher

_____

_____

49

When you have a list of the best go-to people, you have the ability to help others in need. You create connections by being a resource for others. http://aha.pub/RhondaSher

_____

_____

50

Even if you don't think anyone is watching, always present yourself in your best light. Handle yourself in a way that makes people want to be with you. http://aha.pub/RhondaSher

_____

_____

51

Paying it forward by practicing random acts of kindness puts you in a state of joy. You never know when someone will provide you with an unexpected gift of a connection. Joy happens everywhere. http://aha.pub/RhondaSher

_____

_____

52

Connecting with people by listening is extremely important. While in a conversation, use the words, "I hear you," or "I'm hearing you." People who feel heard are more likely to trust and connect with you.
http://aha.pub/RhondaSher

_____

_____

53

Connections are developed by making people smile or laugh. Humor is a great way to break down social barriers, as you invite them to connect with you by showing your humanity and making them feel at ease.
http://aha.pub/RhondaSher

_____

_____

54

Want to make someone's day? Share a valuable resource or a tip about a helpful software application. They will want to reciprocate by sharing something with you.
http://aha.pub/RhondaSher

_____

_____

55

Connecting happens in many ways. When we connect on social media, it's sometimes seen as impersonal. Consider handwriting a note or calling an online connection on the phone. If your intent is to get to know that person, watch the relationship deepen.
http://aha.pub/RhondaSher

_____

_____

56

Pay attention to the amount of time you're talking vs. listening. Connection starts with listening. That is why we have two ears and one mouth. http://aha.pub/RhondaSher

_____

_____

57

Have a specific intention in mind when you approach someone new. People can sense when you are out of integrity with your intention. Remember that nobody wants to be sold to. Be a person of service. http://aha.pub/RhondaSher

_____

_____

58

Support your connections by attending their business events. Just by showing up, you let your connections know that what matters to them is important to you, and you'll be surprised at how many new connections you can make. http://aha.pub/RhondaSher

---

59

We each have our own set of skills and unique perspective to bring to the world. When we connect with people, we enrich each others' lives by sharing our gifts. http://aha.pub/RhondaSher

---

60

You can deepen your connection by giving something away. It can be an article, a card, a small gift, or just your time. It's always about giving. http://aha.pub/RhondaSher

_____

_____

61

People will forget what you said. People will forget what you did, but people will never forget how you made them feel.
-Maya Angelou via http://aha.pub/RhondaSher

_____

_____

An unexpected referral is one of the greatest gifts you can receive from a connection. http://aha.pub/RhondaSher

Rhonda L. Sher
http://aha.pub/ConvertingConnections

Share the AHA messages from this book socially by going to
http://aha.pub/ConvertingConnections.

Section IV

Connect the Dots and Be the Connector

Being a connector pays dividends in so many ways. First, it feels great to help others. Second, by sharing your connections with others, you are helping your connections be successful. That by itself feels good. More importantly, it helps your connections remember you and refer you to their connections. Go the extra mile to be the connector and watch the magic happen.

62

The person with the most connections wins ... every time. -Robin Jay, Award-Winning Filmmaker, President of the Las Vegas Convention Speakers Bureau via http://aha.pub/RhondaSher

_____

_____

63

Connecting with others gives us a sense of inclusion, connection, interaction, safety, and community. Your vibe attracts your tribe, so if you want to attract positive and healthy relationships, be one! -Susan C. Young via http://aha.pub/RhondaSher

_____

_____

64

Connect by sharing referrals. If you know someone who could help one of your connections, make an introduction. Letting someone know you have a resource for them and would be glad to make an introduction is the perfect start. http://aha.pub/RhondaSher

_____

_____

65

Our ability to connect with others is innate, wired into our nervous systems, and we need connection as much as we need physical nourishment. -Sharon Salzberg via http://aha.pub/RhondaSher

_____

_____

66

An unexpected referral is one of the greatest gifts you can receive from a connection. http://aha.pub/RhondaSher

_____

_____

67

Real relationships are the product of time spent with others. Perhaps this is why so many people feel disconnected & yearn for true connection. Invest your time being with people who matter & life will be enriched beyond anything you can imagine. http://aha.pub/RhondaSher

_____

_____

68

When you are introducing two of your connections, make sure everyone feels comfortable. Mention something they both have in common, or bring up a topic to which everyone can contribute.
http://aha.pub/RhondaSher

_____

_____

69

Have a mindset of abundance when it comes to referrals. Get to know people who do what you do, as well as those who complement what you do. You never know when you can help a connection with a great referral. http://aha.pub/RhondaSher

---

70

When you connect with someone, it is important to keep up with them. Nurturing true connections is important because they're based on relationships. Communicating regularly keeps connections alive. http://aha.pub/RhondaSher

---

71

When approaching someone you want to connect with, find something about them that can start a conversation. Then ask open-ended questions to pique interest, and your new connection will give you their attention. http://aha.pub/RhondaSher

_____

_____

72

You start seeing potential relationships everywhere when you become aware of the importance of connections. Instead of taking people in our daily lives for granted, look at the folks in your life for who they are: people like us who have a lot to give. http://aha.pub/RhondaSher

_____

_____

73

We live in a world of connections. It's just a question of whether your eyes are open to seeing all the possibilities.
http://aha.pub/RhondaSher

_____

_____

74

The most important thing in communication is hearing what isn't said. -Peter Drucker
via http://aha.pub/RhondaSher

_____

_____

75

People will go out of their way and do the extraordinary, not the ordinary, when they feel that they are making a contribution. Make it a practice to contribute to someone every day in a positive way. http://aha.pub/RhondaSher

_____

_____

76

Quality connections are about being open to giving and receiving. People love to feel needed and to help others.
http://aha.pub/RhondaSher

_____

_____

77

Take on support roles in networking groups
and watch how easy it is to connect.
http://aha.pub/RhondaSher

_____

_____

78

One of the ways you can be helpful when
connecting with people is asking, "Is there
anybody in my network I can connect you
with?" http://aha.pub/RhondaSher

_____

_____

79

An effective way to create a strong relationship with your online connections is to use Zoom or Skype. Add a personal touch to your online connections. http://aha.pub/RhondaSher

_____

_____

80

When you refer other people to your connections, make sure you know them fairly well. People will judge you by the company you keep, and if a person you refer turns out to be less than stellar, it could damage your credibility. http://aha.pub/RhondaSher

_____

_____

81

Believe in abundance. There is enough money and clients for everyone. When you believe that, you are more likely to be open to sharing and connecting. http://aha.pub/RhondaSher

_____

_____

82

Having good connections is one of the key requirements to having a successful business. @HappyAbout via http://aha.pub/RhondaSher

_____

_____

83

As your sphere of influence expands, your world becomes filled with endless opportunities. You'll be amazed at the seemingly coincidental introductions you receive. Your current connections will refer you to the right person at the right time.
http://aha.pub/RhondaSher

_____

_____

84

Most people do the minimum to keep a connection. Be someone who exceeds expectations. When you exert extra effort for someone, they will want to keep you as a valued connection.
http://aha.pub/RhondaSher

_____

_____

Wherever you are, whomever you meet, notice that there's always a potential new connection right around the corner. People will enter your life as you need them and as they need you. Be open. http://aha.pub/RhondaSher

Rhonda L. Sher
http://aha.pub/ConvertingConnections

Share the AHA messages from this book socially by going to
http://aha.pub/ConvertingConnections.

Section V

Connections Can Appear Anywhere and Everywhere

You don't need to be an extrovert to be successful, but you do need connections to help grow your business. Remember, it's not about who you know but who knows and recommends you. Every connection begins with smiling, listening, and being sincerely interested in other people. Every time you meet someone new, you have an opportunity to make a new connection that will pay off directly or indirectly sometime in the future.

85

Everything is connected. Connections that matter involve being present, listening, and demonstrating to the other person that they matter to you. http://aha.pub/RhondaSher

_____

_____

86

Making connections doesn't have to happen only at big events. It can happen absolutely anywhere. Every place you go, strike up an engaging conversation. Be curious and ask questions. You might make amazing connections in unexpected places. http://aha.pub/RhondaSher

_____

_____

87

A fixation with connecting with "friends" online comes with the risk of disconnection with friends waiting for you to be present in the offline world. -Craig Hodges via http://aha.pub/RhondaSher

_____

_____

88

Connections aren't made merely with a tap of the "like" button. Too often, we approach the computer screen and don't stop to realize there's a person on the other side. Make sure to personalize all your connections. http://aha.pub/RhondaSher

_____

_____

89

Wherever you are, whomever you meet, notice that there's always a potential new connection right around the corner. People will enter your life as you need them and as they need you. Be open. http://aha.pub/RhondaSher

_____

_____

90

Great connections happen in unlikely places. It could be someone from another industry, someone you didn't think would be a good connection. Relationships aren't just one to one, they're one to many. People know those who could use you. Don't pre-judge. http://aha.pub/RhondaSher

_____

_____

91

If you've found the person with whom you'd like to connect, do your homework before reaching out. Look at their website and social media profile. Knowing about their business and interests can help you connect on a deeper level.
http://aha.pub/RhondaSher

92

The way we communicate with others and with ourselves ultimately determines the quality of our lives. I believe that the quality of our lives is directly proportionate to the quality of our connections. -Tony Robbins
via http://aha.pub/RhondaSher

93

The eyes are one of the most powerful tools a woman can have. With one look, she can relay the most intimate message. After the connection is made, words cease to exist. -Jennifer Salaiz via http://aha.pub/RhondaSher

_____

_____

94

If you are truly interested in other people, it's easy to strike up a conversation and find a common area of interest. Open-ended questions are usually the easiest way to start. http://aha.pub/RhondaSher

_____

_____

95

Doing something you'd rather say "no" to can help you grow and make connections you never thought you could have. Go to that networking event or meeting. You never know who you'll meet and what connections you'll make. http://aha.pub/RhondaSher

_____

_____

96

Through my personal connections, I have learned, grown, explored, delighted, discovered, and experienced things I never would have on my own. -Kim Eley, Writing Coach & Publishing Consultant via http://aha.pub/RhondaSher

---

97

You don't have to agree on every topic or issue to connect with someone and form a relationship. http://aha.pub/RhondaSher

---

98

Extend a warm handshake and smile to everyone you meet. Count how many smiles you can give in a single day, and you will be amazed at how many you get back. Smiles are the first step to connecting. http://aha.pub/RhondaSher

_____

_____

99

No one has ever become poor by giving. -Anne Frank. When you give your time, attention, and honest feedback, you should be rewarded with a genuine connection and relationship. http://aha.pub/RhondaSher

_____

_____

100

No matter where you are, you have an opportunity to meet people you can make a connection with. If you nurture it over time, the rewards can be tremendous. It starts with a simple hello. Whom have you connected with today? http://aha.pub/RhondaSher

_____

_____

Connecting is not about driving an instant result. It's a chain of links that will eventually take you where you want to go. Just as no one falls in love on the first date, good business relationships take time and energy.
http://aha.pub/RhondaSher

Rhonda L. Sher
http://aha.pub/ConvertingConnections

Share the AHA messages from this book socially by going to
http://aha.pub/ConvertingConnections.

Section VI

Be Yourself

Some people are naturally good at connecting, and some are not. The good news is that habits such as smiling, acknowledging others, thinking positively, and listening are skills you can practice to be better. The key point is to be you. The real you. The person who can be trusted and who cares about those they interact with.

101

To have meaningful connections with others, you must first be willing to be open with yourself. http://aha.pub/RhondaSher

_____

_____

102

Believe that you have something really valuable to share with people. Your confidence and knowledge will let people know that you are someone who can be trusted and a connection they can count on. http://aha.pub/RhondaSher

_____

_____

103

Fear can keep you from connecting with people, but don't let it win. Take your fear and open it up. There are many great mentors and coaches who can help you tackle your fear and make connections that matter.
http://aha.pub/RhondaSher

104

Having a morning routine that puts you into a mindset for the day is a great way to prepare to connect with others. When you are refreshed from meditation, exercise, or other positive habits, you have an attitude that attracts others.
http://aha.pub/RhondaSher

105

Some people are naturally good at connecting, and some are not. The good news is that habits such as smiling, acknowledging others, thinking positively, and listening are skills you can practice to be better. http://aha.pub/RhondaSher

---

106

Some people ask who they should be when they meet someone new. Should they be overly optimistic, a realist, or adopt the views of the person they're talking to? There's one simple answer: Be Yourself. http://aha.pub/RhondaSher

---

107

Sometimes, we think we're keeping our feelings hidden, but actually, your persona can be easily read by others. To make real connections, think about the way you show up when you meet with someone. http://aha.pub/RhondaSher

---

108

Communication is merely an exchange of information, but connection is an exchange of our humanity. -Sean Stephenson, Get Off Your "But," via http://aha.pub/RhondaSher

109

At conferences and events, there is usually at least one person you can connect with who can provide you with tremendous growth. When you attend the event with this person in mind, you are more likely to connect with them. http://aha.pub/RhondaSher

---

110

When you know who your ideal client or referral partner is, you can strategically attend conferences to make connections with those people. Look for opportunities to expand your sphere of influence. http://aha.pub/RhondaSher

---

111

Arriving at a networking event looking for clients to sell to? Mistake. Smart connectors arrive at networking events ready to make lasting connections. http://aha.pub/RhondaSher

_____ _____

_____

112

Does your picture look outdated or like it was taken at a party? If you're not facing someone in person, your LinkedIn profile picture is your exposure to clients. Make sure your picture looks current and professional so people will want to connect. http://aha.pub/RhondaSher

_____

_____

113

Practice telling people what you
do in a simple and memorable way.
http://aha.pub/RhondaSher

_____

_____

114

Identify master connectors and influencers
and ask to meet with them. They enable you to
meet more people in a shorter amount of time
because they are well-connected.
http://aha.pub/RhondaSher

_____

_____

115

Make sure people know how to contact you. Carry and give out business cards, and make sure your contact info is on your cards, website, and social media posts. People can't connect with you if they can't find you. http://aha.pub/RhondaSher

---

116

Genuine connection works when you're authentic and honest. Connections won't work by trying to be someone you're not. Be yourself when you talk with someone new, and you're more likely to form a lasting connection. http://aha.pub/RhondaSher

---

117

Have you ever tried to walk through a screen door because it looked open but wasn't? The same applies to connecting with people. In order to connect with somebody else, you have to be truly open. http://aha.pub/RhondaSher

_____

_____

118

We strive to appear as our best selves when meeting new people. While you want to make a good impression, relax, take a deep breath, and just be yourself. People connect with others they trust, and people can sense when you are authentic. http://aha.pub/RhondaSher

_____

_____

119

Connecting is not about driving an instant result. It's a chain of links that will eventually take you where you want to go. Just as most people don't fall in love on the first date, good business relationships take time and energy. http://aha.pub/RhondaSher

_____

_____

120

We're given so many opportunities to receive presents, and we often don't see that they're right in front of us. When you have a mindset of gratitude and are thankful for your connections, it seems as though gifts appear from everywhere. http://aha.pub/RhondaSher

_____

_____

121

Connection is why we're here. We are hardwired to connect with others, it's what gives purpose and meaning to our lives, and without it, there is suffering. -Brene Brown via http://aha.pub/RhondaSher

_____

_____

Strive to become a master connector. If you have a circle of people you can refer to, then you become the go-to person. Being that person will increase your connections and bring in more revenue to your business.
http://aha.pub/RhondaSher

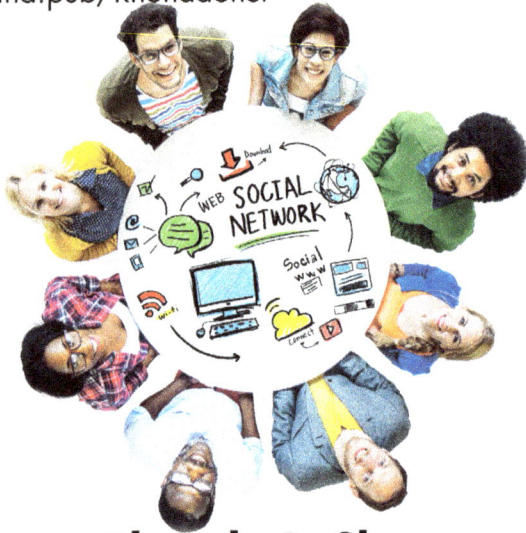

Rhonda L. Sher
http://aha.pub/ConvertingConnections

Share the AHA messages from this book socially by going to
http://aha.pub/ConvertingConnections.

Section VII

Turning Relationships into Revenue

Ultimately in business, we want to make a connection so we can take a relationship to revenue. We want to grow our business, improve our reputation, and establish good standing so we can increase our bottom line. Having good, strong connections will provide many benefits to you over time, including direct and indirect revenue from referrals. Be you, care about the people you're working with, nurture relationships, and look forward to a fun ride.

122

Get off your "ask." You're not going to get it if you don't ask for what you want or need. Don't be timid, speak up. Good connections will want to help you out when you ask. http://aha.pub/RhondaSher

---

123

In order to become financially successful, you need to gain new customers. To meet potential clients, expand beyond your comfort zone and build a circle of people around you. In other words, connect to more people. http://aha.pub/RhondaSher

---

124

People do business with others because they want to, not because they have to. Someone else may do the same thing or sell the same product, but when we genuinely relate to someone, we want to do business with them and introduce them to other people.
http://aha.pub/RhondaSher

125

Don't dismiss a single soul -- you never know who you're talking to, who they might know, or how they might be able to contribute. -Lori Cheek, Founder and CEO of Cheekd and Networkd via http://aha.pub/RhondaSher

126

People take action for one of three reasons: to get out of pain, to seek pleasure, or out of fear of the future. If you can help people with one of these three issues, you will be sought out as an expert and thought leader.
http://aha.pub/RhondaSher

_____

_____

127

A memorable introduction is an in-person experience. If you have an important introduction to make, arrange for both parties to meet with you as the intermediary. Grab coffee, then leave early & give them alone time.
-Brennan White, Cortex
via http://aha.pub/RhondaSher

_____

_____

128

"What can I do for you?" This simple phrase will open doors to connections with the people you want to meet. These are like magic words to obtain what you want or need.
http://aha.pub/RhondaSher

_____

_____

129

A great introduction is incisive, concise, and fun. Ensure both connections know why the introduction is being made in such a way that mutual benefit is apparent.
-Avery Fisher, Remedify,
via http://aha.pub/RhondaSher

_____

_____

130

The best way to develop deep referral relationships is to be unselfish. Ask potential partners, "What are your goals, and how can I help you achieve them?" -Steven David Elliot, CVO Rockstar Connect, RockstarConnect.com via http://aha.pub/RhondaSher

---

131

Strive to become a master connector. If you have a circle of people you can refer to, then you become the go-to person. Being that person will increase your connections and bring in more revenue to your business. http://aha.pub/RhondaSher

132

People don't buy brands. They buy stories. Start telling yours & be your genuine, vulnerable, charming self. The more you connect on a personal level, the more you will be delivering your story & people will buy it.
-Cathy Heller, Entrepreneur,
via http://aha.pub/RhondaSher

133

Invest your time, energy, and attention into building a professional support system for your business. Creating connections is the best way to start. Invest in your connections to receive more value from your business.
http://aha.pub/RhondaSher

134

A great way to make a lasting connection is to be helpful if you can be. I've found that when I offer a piece of advice, some expertise, or make an introduction to a contact, people are thrilled -- more than you'd think.
-Adrian Granzella Larssen
via http://aha.pub/RhondaSher

135

You have to have a generous spirit. The greatest networkers I know genuinely like to help others. They're always doing it. And if they ever do need anything, people will fall over themselves to help them. -Andrew Sobel, "Power Relationships" via http://aha.pub/RhondaSher

136

Getting to know one another & establishing a relationship should be paramount. Once you know & understand each other's strengths, weaknesses, services & needs, then the mutual benefit of the connection will surface. -Carey Green, Business Coach, via http://aha.pub/ RhondaSher

_____

_____

137

Your net worth is only as good
as your network. -Rishi Chowdhury
via http://aha.pub/RhondaSher

_____

_____

138

The highest compliment somebody can give you
from a connection is a referral. Referrals can only
be earned when you have a strong connection.
http://aha.pub/RhondaSher

_____

_____

139

If I want a friend or contact of mine to introduce me to someone, I write the email for them -- this ensures the introduction has all the key talking points. -Luke Skurman, Niche.com via http://aha.pub/RhondaSher

_____

_____

140

Everyone wants to be the five-star choice of their clients. When the people you refer do well, your perception goes up to five stars because of the halo effect: their good service and your referral make you shine.
http://aha.pub/RhondaSher

_____

_____

About the Author

Rhonda Sher is the author of *The Two Minute Networker* (https://amzn.to/2GF6T32), a proven step-by-step guide toward building relationships and growing your business. She is also the author of *The ABC's of LinkedIn, Get LinkedIn or Left Out*, and *52 Ways to Boost Your Business with Business Cards*. She has been speaking, training, and writing about how to leverage LinkedIn for more than a decade.

Rhonda has held key positions in the corporate world, as well as being a successful entrepreneur. Her passion is sharing her knowledge of how to make connections that count, both online and offline, and converting relationships to revenue and profiles to profit.

AHAthat™

AHAthat makes it easy to share, author, and promote content. There are over 40,000 quotes (AHAmessages™) by thought leaders from around the world that you can share in seconds for free.

For those who want to author their own book, we have time-tested proven processes that allow you to write your AHAbook™ of 140 digestible, bite-sized morsels in eight hours or less. Once your content is on AHAthat, you have a customized link that you can use to have your fans/advocates share your content and help grow your network.

➲ Start sharing: https://AHAthat.com

➲ Start authoring: https://AHAthat.com/Author

Rhonda Sher
AHAthat Author

Hey, Did You AHAthat™?

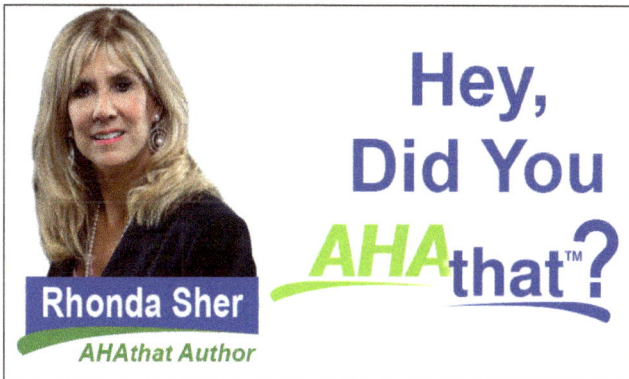

Please go directly to this book in AHAthat and share each AHAmessage socially at
http://aha.pub/ConvertingConnections.